THE Mayflower

by MARK GREENWOOD

illustrated by

FRANÉ LESSAC

Holiday House / New York

The publisher wishes to thank Peter Arenstam,
Plimoth Plantation, for his expert review of this book.

FL wishes to thank Mike Lefroy
for everything nautical.

Library of Congress Cataloging-in-Publication Data
Greenwood, Mark, 1958-
The Mayflower / by Mark Greenwood ; illustrated by Frané Lessac. — First edition.
pages cm
ISBN 978-0-8234-2943-1 (hardcover)
1. Mayflower Compact (1620)—Juvenile literature.
2. Pilgrims (New Plymouth Colony)—Juvenile literature.
3. Mayflower (Ship)—Juvenile literature.
4. Massachusetts—History—New Plymouth, 1620–1691—Juvenile literature.
I. Lessac, Frané, illustrator. II. Title.
F68.G795 2014
974.4'02—dc23
2013011144

For our fathers,
Frank and Arthur

In 1620, the king of England expected his subjects to worship according to the laws of his church. But some people, called Puritans, believed the Church of England was not true to their faith. They prayed in secret, afraid they would be punished if the king found out.

Some Puritans decided to leave England and cross the Atlantic Ocean. Far away, in the New World, they hoped to worship without fear.

Other adventurers, known as Strangers, joined the Puritans on the voyage. Today we call all these travelers Pilgrims.

9

The Pilgrims rowed out to the *Speedwell* and the *Mayflower*—the ships that would transport them across the vast ocean. But water leaked through the *Speedwell's* planking. Some of the passengers decided to abandon the voyage. Others crowded aboard the *Mayflower*.

One hundred and two passengers, including children,
prayed for fair winds when the *Mayflower* sailed alone
on September 6, 1620.

The Pilgrims didn't know what to expect when they
reached their destination. Before them, only explorers and
fishermen had undertaken such a dangerous voyage.

The *Mayflower* was built to carry goods such as wine, textiles, and iron—not people. Between the decks, families were separated for privacy by wooden dividers. They shared the damp, crowded space with chickens, goats, pigs, and two dogs.

Barrels of hard biscuits, beef and fish preserved by salting, casks of cheese, sacks of beans, and gallons of vinegar were stowed in the hold at the bottom of the ship.

15

Before the journey the ship's master, Christopher Jones, had sailed the *Mayflower* only on short trading trips between England and Europe. Now he set a course across thousands of miles of ocean.

Steady winds carried
the *Mayflower* beyond sight
of land. Weeks passed by.

Belowdecks, children listened to stories by lantern light.

After a month at sea, dark clouds gathered on the horizon. October was the start of the stormy season. The wind began to bluster. The ship rose and fell.

The slippery deck was not safe for passengers. But a young man grew restless and stepped out for fresh air. Waves pounded the *Mayflower*'s planking. The ship lurched suddenly, and he tumbled into the sea. John Howland caught a rope trailing from the rigging. The Pilgrims declared it a miracle when the crew hauled him to safety.

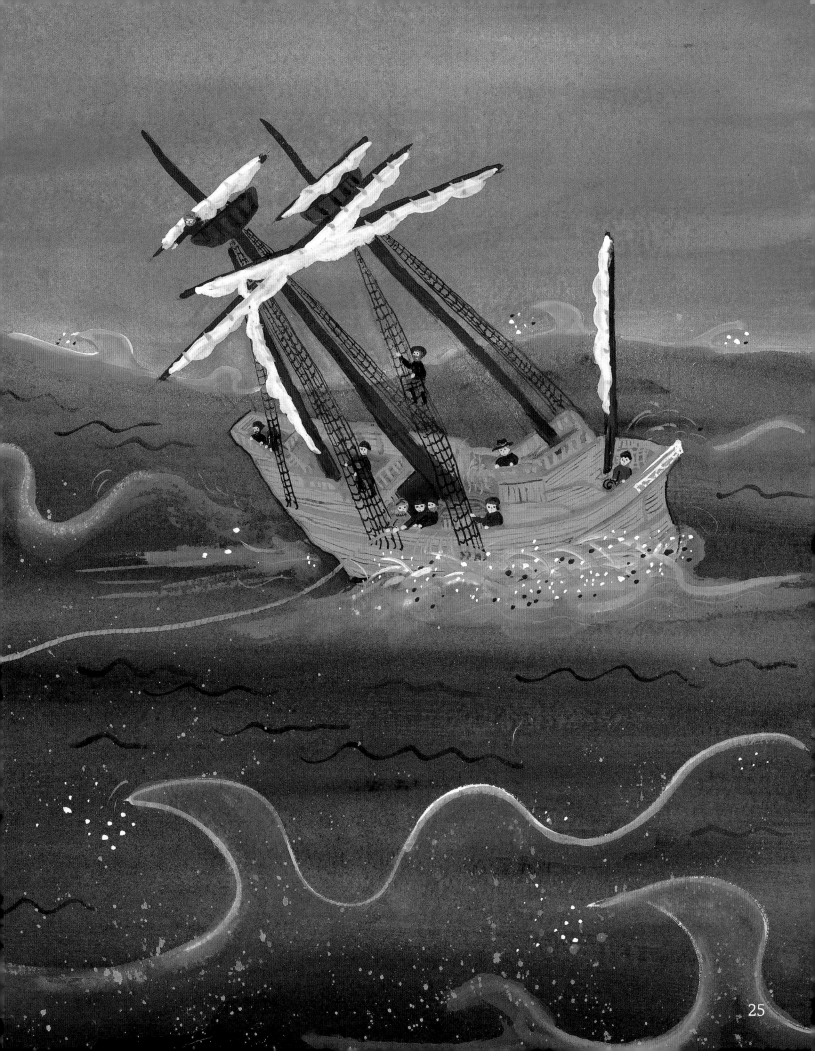

Billowing sails strained the masts. A main beam buckled and cracked. Water poured in, and Master Jones feared the *Mayflower* might sink. Fortunately, the Pilgrims had brought a tool used to lift heavy objects. With the iron screw, the ship's carpenter was able to raise the beam into place.

Finally, the sky cleared and winds calmed. After sixty-five days at sea, many Pilgrims were sick. Two people had died. But at daybreak on November 9, 1620, weary faces smiled at the sight of land on the horizon. Elizabeth Hopkins cradled her son born at sea and named him Oceanus.

Before the Pilgrims set foot ashore, they wrote down laws to govern themselves. Today this document is known as the Mayflower Compact.

Some Pilgrims stayed aboard the ship while others explored the wilderness. By mid-December, they had chosen a place to settle, and the *Mayflower* anchored in Plymouth Harbor. The Pilgrims began building houses, but the snow was thick, and many fell ill that first winter.

On March 16, 1621, a lone Indian approached the settlement. "Welcome, Englishmen," he said. Samoset had learned to speak English from fishermen.

Squanto, another local Indian, came to live with the Pilgrims. He taught them how to plant corn and use fish to fertilize their fields. He introduced them to the powerful Wampanoag leader Massasoit.

Though they had suffered great hardship, the Pilgrims found the freedom they prayed for. On April 5, 1621, Master Jones and his crew bid them farewell. The *Mayflower* set sail, homeward bound for England.

That fall Massasoit and ninety of his warriors joined the Pilgrims for three days of feasting. Together with the Wampanoag, the Pilgrims gave thanks and celebrated their first harvest in the New World.

TIME LINE

September 6, 1620	The *Mayflower* sets sail from Plymouth, England, bound for the New World.
November 9, 1620	The Pilgrims sight land off Cape Cod.
November 11, 1620	The Pilgrims sign the Mayflower Compact.
December 16, 1620	The *Mayflower* arrives in what is now known as Plymouth Harbor.
March 16, 1621	Samoset greets the Pilgrims.
March 21, 1621	Tisquantum (Squanto) meets the Pilgrims.
March 22, 1621	Massasoit, grand Sachem (chief) of the Wampanoag, makes a treaty with the Pilgrims.
April 5, 1621	The *Mayflower* departs for England.
May 6, 1621	The *Mayflower* arrives back in England.
October 3, 1789	President George Washington issues a proclamation setting aside Thursday, November 26, as a day of thanksgiving and prayer.
October 3, 1863	President Abraham Lincoln invites the American people, "with one heart and one voice," to observe the last Thursday of November as a day of Thanksgiving.
December 26, 1941	President Franklin D. Roosevelt signs a bill to establish the fourth Thursday in November as Thanksgiving.

RESOURCES

BOOKS

Bradford, William. *Of Plymouth Plantation*. Original Source: *Bradford's History of Plymouth Plantation, 1606–1646*. Ed. William T. Davis. New York: Charles Scribner's Sons, 1908. http://mith.umd.edu//eada/html/display.php?docs=bradford_history.xml&action=show

Curtin, Ted, and James Baker. *Mayflower II*. Plimoth Plantation. Little Compton: Fort Church Publishers, 1993.

Gebler, Ernest. *The Plymouth Adventure*. New York: Doubleday & Company Inc., 1950.

Heaton, Vernon. *The Mayflower*. Devon, UK: Webb & Bower Ltd., 1980.

Jessup, Edmund. *The Mayflower Story*. Retford, UK: Whartons Ltd., 1977.

Lawton, Wendy. *Almost Home*. Chicago: Moody Publishers, 2003.

Nickerson, Warren Sears. *Land Ho! 1620*. East Lansing: Michigan State University Press, 1997.

Philbrick, Nathaniel. *Mayflower: A story of courage, community and war*. New York: Viking Penguin, 2006.

Plimoth Plantation, Peter Arenstam, John Kemp, and Catherine O'Neill Grace. *Mayflower 1620: A New Look at a Pilgrim Voyage*. Washington DC: National Geographic Children's Books, 2007.

Vinton, Iris. *Boy on the Mayflower*. New York: Scholastic Book Services, 1957.

JOURNALS, PUBLICATIONS, & EDUCATIONAL MATERIALS

Desperate Crossing: The Untold Story of the Mayflower. DVD. The History Channel, 2006.

Journey to the New World. Plimouth Plantation Inc. Educational Materials. Plimouth Plantation, Plymouth, Massachusetts, 2006.

Plimouth Life, 6, no. 1. Plimouth Plantation Publications. Plimoth Plantation, Plymouth, Massachusetts, 2007.